DATE DUE	

PROJECT APOLLO

A TRUE BOOK

by

Diane M. and
Paul P. Sipiera

Ⓟ

Children's Press®
A Division of Grolier Publishing
New York London Hong Kong Sydney
Danbury, Connecticut

An astronaut's footprint on the Moon

Subject Consultant
Peter Goodwin
Science Department Chairman
Kent School, Kent, CT

Reading Consultant
Linda Cornwell
Learning Resource Consultant
Indiana Department
of Education

Authors' Dedication: To our
friends Alan L. Bean,
Apollo 12, and
Harrison H. Schmitt, Apollo 17
—two men who went
to the Moon

Library of Congress Cataloging-in-Publication Data

Sipiera, Diane M.
    Project Apollo / by Diane M. Sipiera and Paul P. Sipiera.
    p. cm. — (A true book)
    Includes bibliographical references and index.
    Summary: Provides a history of the space project to study the moon.
    ISBN 0-516-20435-1 (lib.bdg.)   0-516-26273-4 (pbk.)
    1. Project Apollo (U.S.) —Juvenile literature. [1. Project Apollo
(U.S.)] I. Sipiera, Paul P. II. Title. III. Series.
TL789.8.U6S5674   1997
629.45'4—dc21
                                                                96-38141
                                                                    CIP
                                                                    AC

Contents

The Saturn rocket was developed to launch the Apollo astronauts to the Moon.

From the Earth to the Moon

In 1957, the Soviet Union launched a spacecraft called *Sputnik 1* into orbit around the earth. This began a race between the United States and the Soviet Union to develop rockets and spacecraft that eventually would take people to the Moon. The first person in orbit was Soviet cosmonaut Yuri Gagarin. Later, American astronaut John H. Glenn Jr. also orbited the earth. President John F. Kennedy challenged the United States to place a person on the Moon by the end of the 1960s. The "space race" was on.

The National Aeronautics and Space Administration's (NASA's) plan to place a person on the Moon followed three steps. The first step, Project Mercury (1958–63), tested whether

The Apollo
space capsule

people could live and work in
space. Next, Project Gemini
(1964–66), with two astronauts
on board, developed and tested the spacecraft needed to
go to the Moon. The third
step, Project Apollo (1967–72),
landed people on the Moon.

The Saturn V Rocket

Command module–held the astronauts

Service module–held the power and support systems

Lunar module (inside)–landed on the Moon

Third stage

Second stage

First stage

The Apollo spacecraft, made up of the command module, service module, and lunar module, didn't have enough power to reach outer space on its own. The *Saturn V* rocket was needed for launch.

The *Saturn V* rocket was huge. It was 364 feet (111 meters) long and was made up of three stages, or parts. The first stage and second stage launched the modules into space. The third stage put the spacecraft into orbit around the earth and then on its course to the Moon.

A Tragic Beginning

As Project Gemini was coming to an end, the Saturn rocket that would launch Apollo astronauts to the Moon began to take shape. The first Apollo mission was set for February 21, 1967, with astronauts Virgil (Gus) I. Grissom, Edward H. White II, and Roger Chaffee.

The *Apollo 1* astronauts White, Grissom, and Chaffee died in a tragic accident.

But during training on January 27, there was a terrible accident. An electrical spark inside the spacecraft caused a fireball, and the three astronauts were killed.

The tragedy of *Apollo 1* was a major setback for the space program. Before another mission could be planned, NASA needed to make the spacecraft fireproof. They filled it with a mixture of oxygen and nitrogen

The *Apollo 1* capsule after the fire

11

gas. If a fire broke out, it would not spread as fast as it had in *Apollo 1*, which had been filled with pure oxygen. After three successful launches of the Saturn rocket, NASA was ready to send astronauts on a mission.

Apollo 7 was launched on October 11, 1968, with astronauts Walter M. Schirra Jr., R. Walter Cunningham, and Donn F. Eisele on board. During the ten days that the

The *Apollo 7* astronauts splash down after their successful mission.

spacecraft spent in earth orbit, the astronauts performed almost every procedure needed to get to the Moon. The flight of *Apollo 7* went so well that NASA decided to send *Apollo 8* to the Moon.

Project Apollo

Apollo 7
Eisele, Schirra,
and Cunningham

Apollo 9
McDivitt, Scott,
and Schweickart

Apollo 11
Armstrong, Collins,
and Aldrin

Apollo 13
Lovell, Swigert,
and Haise

Apollo 15
Scott, Worden,
and Irwin

Apollo 17
Schmitt, Evans,
and Cernan

Mission	Astronauts	Launch Date
Apollo 7	Schirra, Eisele, Cunningham	October 11, 1968
Apollo 8	Borman, Lovell, Anders	December 21, 1968
Apollo 9	McDivitt, Scott, Schweickart	March 3, 1969
Apollo 10	Stafford, Young, Cernan	May 18, 1969
Apollo 11	Armstrong, Collins, Aldrin	July 16, 1969
Apollo 12	Conrad, Gordon, Bean	November 14, 1969
Apollo 13	Lovell, Swigert, Haise	April 11, 1970
Apollo 14	Shepard, Roosa, Mitchell	January 31, 1971
Apollo 15	Scott, Worden, Irwin	July 26, 1971
Apollo 16	Young, Mattingly, Duke	April 16, 1972
Apollo 17	Cernan, Evans, Schmitt	December 7, 1972

Practice for a Landing

After *Apollo 7*, the space race reached its peak. It was believed that the Soviets were ready to send a cosmonaut around the Moon. The United States continued with its plan. *Apollo 8* was launched by a *Saturn V* rocket on December 21, 1968, with

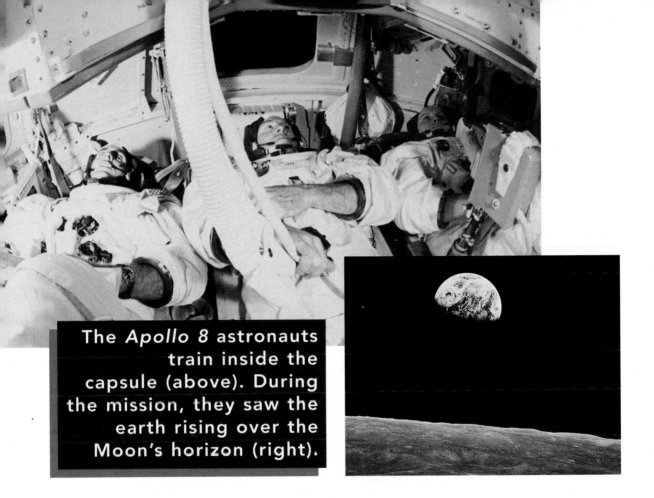

The *Apollo 8* astronauts train inside the capsule (above). During the mission, they saw the earth rising over the Moon's horizon (right).

Frank Borman, James A. Lovell Jr., and William A. Anders as its crew. It reached the Moon on December 24 and orbited it for the next twenty hours. Beneath them, the astronauts saw huge craters and smooth plains. When *Apollo 8* successfully returned to Earth on December 27, the United States was winning the space race.

Before humans could actually land on the Moon, two more missions had to be flown. *Apollo 9* did not fly to the Moon. Instead, it tested the lunar module while in orbit around the earth. The crew was

James A. McDivitt, David R. Scott, and Russell L. Schweickart. For the first time, the astronauts were allowed to name their spacecraft. The command module was called

Apollo 9 stayed in orbit around the earth.

Gumdrop, and the lunar module was named *Spider*. The ten-day mission was a complete success.

Apollo 10 was practice for the first landing. Carrying Thomas P. Stafford, John W. Young, and Eugene A.

Cernan, it was launched on May 18, 1969. The astronauts named their command module *Charlie Brown* and the lunar module *Snoopy*. Once in orbit around the Moon, the lunar

A view of the earth from *Apollo 10*

module and the command module separated, leaving Young alone in the command module. In the lunar module, Stafford and Cernan descended toward the Moon.

Stafford and Cernan flew to within 10 miles (16 kilometers) of the Moon's surface. Then they had to fire their rocket engine and return to the command module. It was not their job to land. That would be left to *Apollo 11*.

"The *Eagle* Has Landed"

The moment the world had waited for came on July 16, 1969, when *Apollo 11* was launched toward the Moon with astronauts Neil A. Armstrong, Michael Collins, and Edwin (Buzz) E. Aldrin Jr.

Once in orbit, the lunar module *Eagle,* carrying

Armstrong and Aldrin, separated from the command module *Columbia.* Collins remained in *Columbia,* orbiting the Moon. There were fearful moments as *Eagle* descended toward the Moon. Its computers overloaded, and Armstrong had to land by flying the spacecraft himself. With less than thirty seconds of fuel left, *Eagle* touched down on its landing site, the Sea of Tranquillity.

When Armstrong stepped off the ladder, he spoke the

Soon after Armstrong announced, "The *Eagle* has landed," the astronauts walked on the Moon for the first time in history.

famous words: "That's one small step for man, one giant leap for mankind." Aldrin joined Armstrong, and they were on the Moon's surface for two hours and thirty-one

HERE MEN FROM THE PLANET EARTH
FIRST SET FOOT UPON THE MOON
JULY 1969, A. D.
WE CAME IN PEACE FOR ALL MANKIND

NEIL A. ARMSTRONG
ASTRONAUT

MICHAEL COLLINS
ASTRONAUT

EDWIN E. ALDRIN, JR.
ASTRONAUT

RICHARD NIXON
PRESIDENT, UNITED STATES OF AMERICA

While they were on the Moon, the astronauts set up science experiments to learn about the new environment (left). This plaque (right) was left on the Moon by *Apollo 11*.

minutes collecting soil and rocks and setting up science experiments. Too soon, it was time to return to *Eagle* and join up with Collins in *Columbia*.

They had fulfilled the dream of reaching another world.

Apollo 11 was soon followed by Apollo 12, launched on November 14, 1969. On board were Charles (Pete) Conrad Jr., Richard F. Gordon Jr., and Alan L. Bean. The highlight of their mission was finding the Surveyor 3 spacecraft. It had been launched in April 1967 to see if landing on the Moon was possible. Scientists were eager to learn what had

Apollo 12 astronaut Pete Conrad works with the *Surveyor 3* spacecraft.

happened to it since its landing. The astronauts removed several parts of the spacecraft for study. In addition, Conrad and Bean collected over 74 pounds (34 kilograms) of rock and made two moonwalks together.

Moon Rocks

The moon rocks collected during the Apollo missions have given scientists a new understanding of how the earth and Moon were formed.

Moon rocks look a lot like the rocks on Earth. But, unlike rocks on Earth, certain types of moon rocks were formed when giant meteorites crashed into the Moon's surface. Some moon rocks are among the oldest material in the solar system.

"Houston, We Have a Problem"

Apollo 13 was launched on April 11, 1970, with James A. Lovell Jr., John L. Swigert Jr., and Fred W. Haise Jr. as its crew. The mission was going as planned until an explosion shook the spacecraft. *Apollo 13* lost power and oxygen. The astronauts reported the dan-

ger to Mission Control in Texas, "Houston, we have a problem." The astronauts' lives were at risk, and the moon landing had to be canceled. The most important thing was to get the astronauts back alive.

Apollo 13 did not land on the Moon, but it did take pictures as it passed.

NASA scientists and engineers came up with many ideas to help the crew. First, they had the astronauts move from the command module to the lunar module, which had not been damaged in the explosion. It took great courage and skill for the astronauts to survive. They made it back to Earth just before their oxygen supply ran out. It was Lovell's second trip to the Moon without landing, but he was happy just to be alive.

Four More Missions

Project Apollo quickly recovered after the *Apollo 13* crisis. The next mission, *Apollo 14*, was launched on January 31, 1971, with Alan B. Shepard Jr., Stuart A. Roosa, and Edgar D. Mitchell. They landed where *Apollo 13* was supposed to have set down. Shepard and Mitchell conducted many experiments and collected

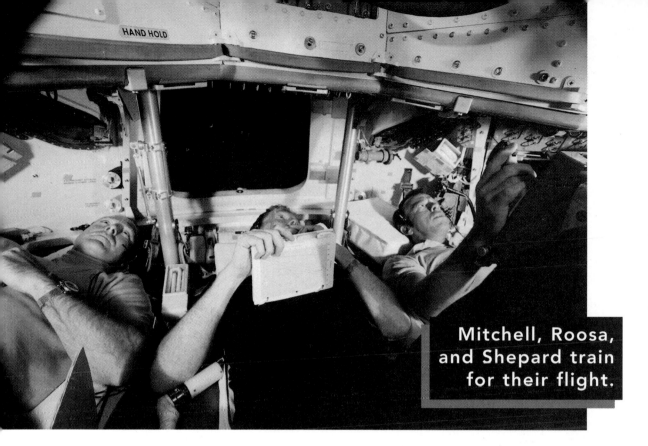

HAND HOLD

Mitchell, Roosa, and Shepard train for their flight.

rock samples during their two moonwalks. Shepard was not only America's first person in space during Project Mercury, but he became the first person ever to hit a golf ball on the Moon!

The lunar rover allowed the astronauts to travel farther from their lunar module to collect interesting rocks.

The next mission was launched on July 26, 1971. *Apollo 15* carried astronauts David R. Scott, Alfred M. Worden, and James B. Irwin. It was the first mission to use a lunar rover, a small car designed to help the astronauts explore farther away from the lunar module.

As experience with landings grew, Mission Control looked for more challenging landing sites. *Apollo 16* was sent to the mountains of the Moon to look for some of the oldest moon rocks. It was launched on April 16, 1972, with astronauts John W. Young, Thomas K. Mattingly II, and Charles M. Duke Jr. on board. With their lunar rover, Young set a speed record of 11 miles (18 km) per hour.

Although *Apollo 14, 15,* and *16* were all successful, the United States decided to cancel its moon program—due to cost and the loss of public interest—and focus on new projects. *Apollo 17* would be the last moon mission.

Geologist Harrison H. Schmitt, selected to join Eugene A. Cernan and Ronald E. Evans in the crew, collected many impor- tant rock samples. Schmitt's descriptions of what he saw were also a help to scientists on Earth.

Apollo 17 accomplished its mission. As Cernan climbed into

Cernan and Evans float in *Apollo 17* (left). Cernan planted the U.S. flag on the Moon's surface (above).

the lunar module, he became
the last Apollo astronaut to walk
on the Moon.

Project Apollo

Much was accomplished by Project Apollo. The most important achievement was simply getting humans to the Moon and bringing them back safely. That is what most people will remember.

For the scientists, more than 800 pounds (363 kg) of

Rocks from the Moon (left)
are delivered to a research
laboratory (right).

moon rocks were collected.
They have taught scientists a
lot about the origin of the
earth and Moon. For the
United States, Project Apollo
brought people together.

Everyone took pride in their country as Neil Armstrong set foot on the Moon.

The project also helped bring the Soviets and Americans together. In July 1975, the United States and the Soviet Union launched a joint mission named the Apollo-Soyuz Test Project. The *Apollo 18* spacecraft linked up with the *Soyuz 19* spacecraft in space, and the Soviet cosmonauts shook hands with the American

The Soviet and U.S. crews of the Apollo-Soyuz mission

astronauts. It was a small step toward cooperation in space exploration. The space race had finally come to an end.

To Find Out More

Here are more places to learn about space exploration:

 **Books**

Charleston, Gordon.
Armstrong Lands on the Moon. Macmillan, 1994.

Kennedy, George P. **Apollo to the Moon.** Chelsea House, 1992.

Sipiera, Diane M. and Paul P. **Project Gemini.** Children's Press, 1997.

Stein, R. Conrad. **Apollo 11.** Children's Press, 1992.

Sullivan, George. **The Day We Walked on the Moon.** Scholastic, 1990.

Vogt, Gregory. **Apollo and the Moon Landing.** Millbrook, 1991.

 **Organizations**

The Planetary Society
65 North Catalina Avenue
Pasadena, CA 91106
(818) 793-5100
http://planetary.org/tps/

NASA Teacher Resource Center
Mail Stop 8-1
NASA Lewis Research Center
21000 Brookpark Road
Cleveland, OH 44135
(216) 433-4000

National Air and Space Museum
Smithsonian Institution
601 Independence Avenue SW
Washington, DC 20560
(202) 357-1300

Online Sites

The Children's Museum of Indianapolis
http://childrensmuseum. org/sq1.htm

Visit the SpaceQuest Planetarium to see what it has to offer, including a view of this month's night sky. It can connect you to other astronomy Web sites, too.

History of Space Exploration
http://bang.lanl.gov/ solarsys/history.htm

This site has a helpful time-line of space exploration and tells the history of the spacecraft and astronauts.

Kid's Space
http://liftoff.msfc.nasa.gov/ kids/welcome.html

Space exploration is really fun at this Web site. Find out how much you would weigh on the Moon, play games, solve puzzles, take quizzes, read stories, and look at the gallery of pictures drawn by kids. Find out how you can post a drawing online, too!

NASA Home Page
http://www.nasa.gov

Visit NASA to access information about its exciting history and present resources.

The Nine Planets
http://seds.lpl.arizona.edu/ nineplanets/nineplanets/ nineplanets.html

Take a multimedia tour of the solar system and all of its planets and moons.

Space Telescope Science Institute
http://www.stsci.edu/

The Space Telescope Science Institute is in charge of operating the Hubble Space Telescope. Visit this site to see pictures of the telescope's outer-space view.

Important Words

command module the part of the spacecraft that carries the astronauts during space travel

crater a bowl-shaped landform

geologist a scientist who studies rocks, minerals, and landforms

lunar module the part of the spacecraft designed to land on the Moon

mission a goal for spacecraft or astronauts to accomplish

Mission Control the center in charge of ground communications and operations during a mission

moonwalk walking on the Moon

orbit the path a spacecraft travels around the earth or Moon

plains flat areas of land

rocket a powerful vehicle that launches capsules into space

Index

Meet the Authors

Paul and Diane Sipiera are a husband and wife who share interests in nature and science. Paul is a professor of geology and astronomy at William Rainey Harper College in Palatine, Illinois. He is a member of the Explorers Club, the New Zealand Antarctic Society, and was a member of the United States Antarctic Research Program. Diane is the director of education for the Planetary Studies Foundation of Algonquin, Illinois. She also manages and operates the STARLAB planetarium program for her local school district.

When they are not studying or teaching science, Diane and Paul can be found enjoying their farm in Galena, Illinois, with their daughters, Andrea, Paula Frances, and Carrie Ann.